Personal Finance in a Gig Economy

Strategies for Modern Workers

Table of Contents

Chapter 1. Introduction

Welcome to an illuminating Special Report that shines a spotlight on the world of personal finance, with a keen focus on the ebbs and flows of today's gig economy! As we navigate the exciting waters of modern-day employment, traditional financial strategies often fall short. This report expertly equips modern workers, freelancers, contractors, and temporary workers with unique strategies to turn uncertainties into opportunities. Bursting with valuable insights, top-notch advice from experts, and practical resources, our report is all set to empower you to take control of your finances and thrive in the gig economy. Get ready to transform your financial life with innovative tools, tips, and tactics that will surely motivate and inspire. Get yourself a copy today and make your journey in the gig economy as prosperous as it can be!

Chapter 2. The Rise of the Gig Economy

To truly understand the complexities of today's financial landscape, one must comprehend the rise of the gig economy, its driving factors, and its implications. This phenomenon has influenced how people approach employment, challenging the status quo and encouraging a new realm of creativity, flexibility, and entrepreneurial spirit.

2.1. The Dawn of a New Era

The gig economy began to gain prominence in the late 2000s following the global financial crisis. Many found themselves without traditional employment and began looking for alternative working arrangements. This created a ripe environment for gig economy platforms, such as Uber and Airbnb, to blossom. These platforms acted as intermediaries, connecting individuals offering services with those requiring them.

At the same time, advancements in technology were disrupting traditional industries. The internet and smart devices became widespread, and digital platforms sprung to life, making it easier than ever for workers and employers to connect in real-time. This technology-driven connectivity facilitated the exchange of gig-based services.

2.2. The Millennial Factor

Examining the demographics, millennials, who prioritize work-life balance, flexibility and personal freedom considerably over job security, were drawn towards the gig economy. The traditional 9 to 5 employment model of their predecessors seemed less attractive to them. A report by Deloitte showed more than 70% of millennials see themselves working independently at some point rather than being employees within traditional organizational structures.

2.3. An Economy of Scale

The gig economy flourished due to its ability to offer services at scale. Whether it was a freelancer offering their coding skills to multiple companies or a ride-share driver providing transport to numerous commuters, the traditional employment model, focusing on one job and one employer, was challenged. This brought an economy of scale, with gig workers potentially earning more through providing services to multiple "employers" and consumers benefiting from lower prices than traditional models could offer.

2.4. The Power of Technology

The digital age played an instrumental role in the rise of the gig economy. Platforms such as Upwork or Fiverr have redefined the nature of work by simplifying the process of connecting gig workers with those who need their services. Mobile technology, cloud computing, and automation tools have enhanced productivity and removed geographical restrictions, further propelling the gig economy.

2.5. Regulatory Challenges

While the gig economy has seen swift growth, it has also faced regulatory challenges. Questions about worker rights, employment classification, and taxation have emerged. Many countries and states are grappling with legislation to protect gig economy workers without stifling the innovation that has benefited millions.

2.6. The COVID-19 Accelerant

The exponential boom of the gig economy was further magnified by the COVID-19 pandemic, as traditional in-person jobs dwindled. The need for physical distancing and quarantine measures resulted in an unprecedented demand for remote work and services. Airbnb hosts turned their short-term rentals into remote workspaces, while delivery services, such as Uber Eats and DoorDash, saw explosive growth.

2.7. The Future of Work: Decentralised and Dispersed

Today's gig economy is on the cusp of achieving new milestones with the advent of blockchain and cryptocurrency. On the one hand, the gig economy is becoming more organized and efficient with blockchain-based contracts offering transparency, security, and operational effectiveness. On the other, cryptocurrency is offering gig workers a seamless way to engage in cross-border contracts without having to navigate conventional banking issues.

As we navigate through the 21st century, the gig economy's rise shows no signs of slowing. As such, understanding how this economy works is crucial to equipping ourselves for a future where work is decentralized, dispersed, and increasingly digital. It's more important than ever to adapt our personal financial strategies to thrive within this dynamic.

Chapter 3. Establishing Your Financial Foundation

The gig economy is a fast-paced and fluid environment, one where earnings can vary drastically from one day to the next, one month to the next, or even one gig to the next. Such fluctuations call for a strong financial foundation to maintain stability amidst this volatility.

3.1. Building an Emergency Fund

The unpredictable nature of gig work necessitates an emergency fund. This is a cash reserve that you can easily access in times of unplanned expenses or if your income takes a dip.

Financial experts commonly advise setting aside three to six months' worth of living expenses. However, considering the uncertainty of the gig economy, you might want to aim for a more significant safety net, say, nine to twelve months. Here are some steps to building your emergency fund:

1. Determine your monthly living expenses.

2. Set a savings goal based on the amount you've decided to set aside.

3. Create a dedicated savings account.

4. Build the fund gradually. Don't rush; consistent, small deposits can accumulate quickly.

Remember, your emergency fund should be readily accessible, but not so accessible that you're tempted to dip into it for non-emergency expenses.

3.2. Budgeting Wisely

Even more so than in traditional employment, budgeting is essential for gig workers. Since your income varies, your budget should be flexible and responsive to changes. Here are some key points:

1. Assess your high and low income months. Plan for the worst-case scenario and ensure you can cover your basic needs in leaner periods.

2. Split your expenses into fixed (like rent, utilities) and variable costs (like dining out, entertainment). Cut back on variable expenses in lower-income months.

3. Avoid unnecessary debt. Given the prospect of unpredictable earning months, accruing debt can create added pressure.

3.3. Debt Management Tactics

Debt can quickly become unmanageable in the gig economy if not properly addressed. But, with smart strategies, you can keep your debt under control.

1. Prioritize your debts. Pay off higher interest loans first to minimize the total interest you end up paying.

2. Consolidate your debts if possible. Debt consolidation can simplify your payments and potentially lower interest rates.

3. Avoid taking on more debt to pay off existing debt. This is a vicious cycle that can lead to financial ruin.

3.4. Investing for the Future

With all the uncertainties in your career, it's easy to overlook your future financial needs. However, establishing an investment strategy is critical for your long-term financial health.

1. Start saving for retirement as early as possible. Even small, consistent contributions can accumulate over time.

2. Consider multiple income streams. Invest in assets like bonds, stocks, or real estate that generate passive income.

3. Don't put all your eggs in one basket. Diversity minimizes risk since different investments respond differently to market fluctuations.

4. Consult with a financial advisor to create a customized investment strategy.

3.5. Tax Planning

Tax management can be particularly challenging in the gig economy. This is largely because you're responsible for tracking your earnings and calculating your own taxes. Here are some tips:

1. Keep immaculate records. Keep track of your income, expenses, and mileage if your work involves driving.

2. Understand your tax obligations. Gig workers are typically considered self-employed, meaning you'll probably have to file quarterly estimated tax payments.

3. Consider hiring a tax consultant. Navigating tax laws can be tricky, and a professional can help you both understand and reduce your tax liability.

3.6. Managing Health and Other Risks

As a gig worker, you may not have access to traditional employment benefits like health insurance. Consequently, addressing such needs requires further financial planning.

1. Research and invest in a suitable health insurance plan. There's a vast array of private plans available, so take time to understand what fits your needs.

2. Consider disability and life insurance. As the sole provider, you need to ensure both you and anyone dependent on you are covered.

As you press ahead in the gig economy, remember that building a solid financial foundation is not an overnight ordeal but a continuous process rooted in astute planning and deliberate steps. Nurture good habits like regular saving, sensible budgeting, wise investing, and effective risk management, and you'll create a resilient financial platform that can weather uncertainties and optimize opportunities.

Chapter 4. Personal Finance Tools for Gig Workers

Despite being part of a significant workforce shift, gig workers often find themselves navigating the tumultuous waters of financial management unaided. The need for a toolbox filled with robust personal finance management tools has never been more crucial. Amid income irregularities, tax complications, unexpected expenses, and an ever-evolving financial landscape, gig workers must be more vigilant with their financial planning to foster a sense of economic security.

4.1. Budgeting Essentials for Gig Economy

First and foremost in your toolbox should be the essential budgeting tools to help you keep track of your earnings, expenses, and in particular, the variability that comes with gig work. Ranging from simplicity to complexity, several tools exist that can help you craft a budget that suits your needs.

A simple spreadsheet solution such as Google Sheets or Microsoft Excel can be customized to fit your specific needs. Spreadsheets present an unstructured way to manage your finances and allow you to detail your income and expenses as specifically as you would like.

However, there are also numerous budgeting apps such as Mint, YNAB (You Need A Budget), and PocketGuard. These apps can integrate directly with your bank accounts and credit cards, compile your transactions in one place, and categorize your spending for you. Furthermore, they often provide helpful visual aids such as charts and graphs, offer advice on saving, and can even help forecast future income and expenses.

4.2. Invoicing and Payment Tools

As a gig worker, sending invoices and getting paid in a timely manner is of utmost importance. Tools like Wave, FreshBooks, and Quickbooks provide invoicing solutions designed to fit the needs of freelancers and small businesses. Employing these options will allow you to track your client work, generate professional invoices, and avoid falling into the trap of disorganized finances.

Some new tools also offer the ability to directly receive payments through their platform, helping to streamline the income process. PayPal, Venmo, and Zelle are such examples.

4.3. Expense Tracking: Avoiding the Unexpected

Track your expenses carefully to master your cash flow. This step is especially important for gig workers due to the irregular nature of their income. Applications like Expensify, Zoho Expense, and QuickBooks Self Employed can track expenses, categorize them, and even help to automate your expense reporting.

The automation allows you to focus less on the manual labour of entering data and spend more time working and earning. Importantly, these tools often have the added benefit of helping track business expenses for tax purposes.

4.4. Saving and Investment Tools

Planning for the future in the gig economy often means taking saving and investing into your own hands. Robo-advisors and "micro-investing" apps are becoming more popular among gig workers for their ease of use, low costs, and the ability to start with small sums of money.

Robo-advisors, like Betterment and Wealthfront, build and manage a diversified portfolio for you to meet your personal financial goals. Micro-investing tools, like Acorns or Stash, round up your daily transactions to invest the spare change automatically.

An interesting tool for gig workers looking to save for retirement is Honest Dollar. This tool allows gig workers to set up individual retirement accounts (IRAs) that suit their needs, providing a platform to save for the future in spite of an unpredictable income.

4.5. Tax Management Tools

In the gig economy, underestimating or mismanaging your tax obligations can lead to big headaches down the line. Several tools can simplify this process by helping you save for tax payments, estimating what you owe, and help you file your taxes.

Quickbooks Self-Employed helps you track income, expenses, mileage, and estimate your quarterly taxes. Other solutions like TurboTax, H&R Block, and Freelancer Tax Bundle offer additional services to aid in filing taxes, maximizing deductions, and ensuring your tax season goes as smoothly as possible.

In conclusion, managing personal finances as a gig worker could be a tall order. However, with these tools at your disposal, you can better organize your financial life and carve a prosperous path amidst the unpredictable waves of the gig economy. Opting for the tools that best resonates with your needs and integrating them in your daily financial practices will surely enhance your ability to sustainably navigate the uncertain yet thrilling world of gig work.

Chapter 5. Creating a Budget That Works for You

Budgeting sits at the core of sound financial management. Often cast in a rather drab, restrictive light, it instead deserves to be celebrated as a powerful tool for freedom, autonomy, and opportunity, especially in the mercurial landscape of the gig economy. A thoughtfully constructed budget not only equips you to weather financial storms but also enables you to seize advantageous opportunities – a trait highly valuable for any gig-worker. In this comprehensive guide, we'll take you through every step of creating a budget tailor-made to your unique needs and realities.

5.1. Understanding Your Income

The first step towards creating a budget suited to the gig economy is to fully understand your income. Since your earnings are likely to fluctuate, it's crucial to have a good grasp of your income patterns. Monitor your income for a few months to discern trends.

For instance, if you are a freelance copywriter, you might note that you get more jobs during certain months, like the first few months of the year when businesses are planning their strategies. You could then adjust your budget to account for months where you may have fewer jobs.

Another critical factor in understanding your income is your tax obligations. In contrast to traditional employment, gig workers are responsible for their own taxes, such as self-employment tax, Social Security, Medicare, and, in some cases, state and local taxes. Be sure to account for these liabilities.

5.2. Distinguishing Needs from Wants

An essential step in constructing a working budget is differentiating between necessities and luxuries. Needs are items or services that you cannot live without, such as housing, food, transportation, health care, and minimum debt payments.

Wants, on the other hand, include items or services that enhance your lifestyle but aren't essential survival necessities. Examples may include a Netflix subscription, dining out, vacations, and more. Once you understand the distinction between your needs and wants, you can prioritize your spending accordingly.

5.3. Making Your Money Work for You

In the gig economy, it's particularly important that each dollar you earn works as hard as possible for you. Here are a few strategies to make this happen:

1. Regularly Review Your Spending: Keep track of all your expenses, including even minor ones. Review them regularly to understand where your money is going, making cutbacks in discretionary areas if necessary.

2. Negotiate Regular Bills: Make it a habit to review and negotiate regular bills — insurance premiums, mobile plans, Internet packages — to yield some savings.

3. Invest In Tools To Boost Productivity: Invest in tools and equipment that enhance your productivity, enabling you to earn more.

5.4. Planning for Uncertainty

One of the most efficient ways to deal with income uncertainties in the gig economy is by maintaining an emergency fund. The typical recommendation is having three to six months' worth of living expenses, set aside as a cash cushion that can support you during lean periods.

Simultaneously, it's wise to invest in disability and income protection insurance. As an independent gig worker, your income may cease if you're unable to work. Having a safety net in place could be invaluable.

5.5. Saving for the future

Despite the less predictable income, gig workers must not neglect long-term financial goals, such as retirement. Identify retirement schemes that cater to your specific situation, like a SEP IRA or a Solo 401(K) for the self-employed, and budget to contribute regularly.

5.6. Revisiting and reassessing your budget

Finally, keep in mind that a budget is not a static document but an evolving tool. Regularly reassess your budget, incorporating new information, and iterating when necessary.

Creating a budget that works for you in a gig economy can seem daunting initially. However, once you understand the nuances of your income, learn to differentiate your needs from wants, and make your money work harder for you, the path becomes clearer. Embrace the uncertainty, prepare for eventualities, and save for the long term, because your budget is not a set of restrictions, but your ticket to financial peace and prosperity in a dynamic and rewarding gig economy.

Chapter 6. Optimizing Income Streams

The gig economy is a contemporary, flexible, and volatile field that elicits the need for proactive financial strategies. The process of reaching financial equilibrium and success relays back to streamlining and optimizing income flow.

6.1. Identifying Potential Income Streams

Successful navigation in the gig economy begins with identifying potential income streams. As a gig worker, you can generate revenue from one gig or diversify, by engaging in several gigs simultaneously. Typically, a diversified income stream is more stable and secure, as it minimizes your dependency on one source.

Know your skills and discern how you can use them to generate income. Are you a skilled graphic designer, a strong writer, or a gifted language tutor? Consider using these skills on platforms such as Fiverr, Upwork, or Preply. Keep an eye out for emerging new platforms, as they often need early adopters and offer lucrative deals.

In digital times, harness the power of the internet through social media endorsements, online courses, or e-books, adding to your revenue generation.

6.2. Robust Financial Planning

Working in the gig economy requires a robust financial plan.

1. Prioritize Your Earnings: Outline your primary and secondary income sources. Your primary earnings should meet your basic

needs (housing, food, utilities), while secondary earnings can contribute to savings or a retirement fund.

2. Budgeting: Create a budget, factoring in both your income and expenses. Include the irregular income streams and potential dry spells. Stay flexible with your budgets - it's more a guideline than a rule.

3. Rainy Day Fund: A contingency plan is vital. Your rainy day fund should be substantial enough to cover between three to six months' worth of expenditures. This reserve will help in case of unexpected expenses or an unforeseen decrease in income.

4. Insurance: Purchase health and disability insurance. In case of a health emergency, this precaution can make all the difference.

5. Retirement Planning: Unlike traditional employees, gig workers need to plan and contribute to their retirement funds independently. Consult financial advisors and take advantage of customized plans suited to your needs.

6.3. Maximizing Gig Economy Opportunities

With the right strategies, you can maximize your income from gig employment.

1. Upskilling and Cross-Skilling: Regular upskilling and cross-skilling help you diversify your income. Learn new skills relevant to a broader range of clients or improve your existing skills to command higher pay.

2. Networking: Connect with professionals in your field. Attend networking events and make meaningful connections to secure more contracts and learn about potentially lucrative opportunities.

3. Reputation: Maintain a solid reputation for reliability and quality.

Satisfied clients are likely to provide referrals and repeat business.

4. Seasonal Gigs: Look out for seasonal gigs that pay more due to high demand. Plan your schedule to accommodate these gigs and increase your income.

5. Self-Promotion: Actively promote yourself through social media platforms and freelancing websites. Showcase your portfolio, share customer testimonials, and effectively market your skills.

6.4. Negotiating Your Worth

Don't undermine your self-worth in the gig landscape; remember to negotiate your pay reasonably. Identify industry benchmarks for your services, quantify the value you add, consider the time, effort, and resources, and negotiate accordingly. Avoid working for exposure or promises; always seek fair compensation for your skills and time.

6.5. Tax Planning

Freelancers, unlike full-time employees, have to deal with complex tax fillings. It's critical to understand the nature of your income, the deductions available, and the deadlines involved.

1. Get to Grips with Your Taxes: Understand the tax implications of your work. Consult a tax advisor if necessary, to leverage tax deductions.

2. Stay Organized: Keep an accurate record of your income and expenses. Online tools like QuickBooks or Expensify can simplify this process.

3. Pay Estimated Taxes: Since employers don't withhold taxes for freelancers, you'll need to estimate your annual tax liability and pay in quarterly installments.

4. Utilize Retirement Accounts: Funds placed into retirement accounts such as an individual retirement account (IRA) or solo 401(k) can be tax-deductible.

Learning the ropes of the gig economy can be daunting. However, with the right practices and strategies, you can not only survive but thrive, leading a financially secure and comfortable life. Approaching the volatile market with financial intelligence will bring fruitful rewards, making every risk well worth its while. Girding oneself with these practices will reduce the dread of liquidity crises and improve your financial health.

Remember, in the gig economy, there is no linear trajectory to success; the power to shape your career and finances is indeed in your hands. Seeing through the fog of uncertainty demands adaptability, strategic planning, constant learning, and above all, bravery.

Chapter 7. Managing Healthcare and Retirement

Healthcare and retirement may seem like two planets orbiting in distant galaxies when you're engaged in the thrilling and unpredictable world of the gig economy. With erratic schedules, inconsistent earnings, and the liberty of control, traditional models for healthcare and retirement planning simply don't fit in. However, a strategic overhaul unveils a plethora of possibilities that could map your pathway to a well-secured life. Buckle up, as we take you through an expedition to decode the enigma of managing healthcare and retirement in the modern gig economy.

7.1. The Challenge of Healthcare

The traditional full-time employment package usually comes with employer-sponsored health insurance. However, gig workers are typically on their own. Without an employer's contribution, healthcare often becomes exorbitantly expensive and complicated. The escalating healthcare costs could indeed act as a deterrent, but abandoning healthcare is a gamble too big to take. Astute planning and a careful choice of options offer a way out.

First, check out for eligibility in the public health insurance general programs like Obamacare, Medicaid or Medicare. The Affordable Care Act (ACA), colloquially known as Obamacare, offers health insurance to millions of Americans, and the premiums are dependent on one's income levels. You may also be eligible for tax credits which could make the healthcare plan more affordable.

Secondly, you could consider direct primary care, where you pay a flat monthly fee directly to a physician for a range of services, which keeps costs transparent and often lower.

Lastly, health sharing plans are collaborative programs, where the members share each other's healthcare costs. They aren't insurance but can be effective, particularly for those in good health.

7.2. The Retirement Maze

Retirement is an essential consideration that gig economy workers can't afford to overlook. Herein the absence of an employer-led retirement plan, like the common 401(k), doesn't mean you should dismiss the scheme of earning during non-earning days.

It is possible to set up retirement plans as self-employed individuals. Solo 401(k) or Individual 401(k), Simplified Employee Pension (SEP) IRA and Savings Incentive Match Plan for Employees (SIMPLE) IRA are some of the best options that come with high contribution limits and tax advantages.

Choose which plan fits your needs best depending on how much you can contribute, your income levels, and whether you have employees. The rule of thumb is to start early and let the power of compounding work its magic.

7.3. Factoring in The Golden Years

As we move towards the next half of our journey try exploring some strategies that involve factoring in your golden years while thriving in the gig economy. You need to understand that traditional age markers might not hold true in your case. The gig economy, for all its freedom, offers no clear retirement age. This translates to the freedom of extending your working years and intentionally designing your retirement.

Consider gradually tapering off your gig work, building a semi-retirement phase. This approach will also let you test the retirement waters before you plunge completely. If you love your gig, it's okay to keep it going! What you aim for is financial stability and the freedom to choose, rather than the cessation of work.

7.4. Financial Tools and Techniques

Now comes the exciting part - the gadgets in your financial toolkit. To effectively manage your healthcare and retirement, you have to fiddle around with budgeting tools, savings strategies, and investment avenues.

A crucial strategy would be to set your budgets with variable income in mind. Prioritize your healthcare and retirement payments and work the rest of your budget around them.

Consider maintaining an emergency fund distinct from your retirement savings, as dipping into the latter can bring hefty penalties. Have around 6-8 months of living expenses in your emergency stash.

Don't shy away from technology. Tools like Mint.com for budgeting, HealthSherpa for navigating the ACA health insurances, or blooom for managing your self-directed retirement accounts, can be incredibly helpful.

To summarize, managing healthcare and retirement as a gig economy worker might not be a cakewalk, but it's definitely not an uphill battle with no respite either. What you need is the right piece of the puzzle in place, a good measure of patience, and the will to experiment. So, let's brave this new world and rewrite the rules to fit our narrative. Secure your healthcare plans and nest your golden eggs early. After all, it's your well-earned money and you have all the right to secure it your way. Embrace the flexibility and the sense of control that comes with it. Your journey in the gig economy ought to be as prosperous as can be!

Chapter 8. Handling Taxes in a Gig Economy

From understanding tax obligations to strategically maximizing deductions, handling taxes in a gig economy can seem like traversing a maze without a roadmap. However, with the appropriate knowledge, guidance, and strategies, it's possible to navigate this realm with confidence and ease.

8.1. Understanding Your Tax Obligations

When operating within the gig economy, it's essential to understand that you are considered self-employed by the tax authorities. This means that you are responsible for paying both income tax and self-employment tax (Social Security and Medicare). The latter is typically withheld by an employer in traditional employment, but in the gig economy, the responsibility lies solely with you.

As a general rule, if you earn more than $600 from one platform or client in a year, they will send you a 1099 form which you use when filing your taxes. However, any income, regardless of the amount, is considered taxable. Don't fall into the trap of thinking that if you didn't receive a 1099 form, you don't need to report that income. Always keep careful track of your gig income so you can accurately report it when tax season comes round.

8.2. Organizing Your Records

Proper organization of your financial records is key to successfully managing your taxes in the gig economy. Maintain a distinct separation between your personal and work-related transactions.

Consider having a separate bank account for your work income and expenses. This will make tracking and reporting your income and expenses significantly easier.

Regularly updating your records helps to avoid the last-minute rush. Make a habit of consistently recording your income and expenses. There are numerous apps and software platforms that can facilitate this process, such as QuickBooks, Wave, or Mint.

8.3. Utilizing Expense Deductions

As a gig worker, you have the advantage of claiming various work-related expenses as tax deductions. Common examples can include equipment, home office setups, transport costs for work, and even certain meals and entertainment expenses. Remember, only expenses that are necessary and ordinary to carry on the trade or business can qualify.

Documenting these expenditures is crucial - keep all your receipts. It's also a good practice to note down why the expense was necessary for your business, to help recall the function of the expense if you're ever audited.

8.4. Quarterly Estimated Taxes

As a gig economy worker, you may also have to consider the responsibility of paying quarterly estimated taxes. These are a series of four tax payments that you make to the IRS throughout the year. The IRS requires that taxes should be paid as you earn or receive income, not just at the end of the year.

Staying on top of this requirement can help you avoid underpayment penalties at the end of the year. Make dates with these deadlines, typically the 15th of April, June, September, and January, to ensure you don't fall behind.

8.5. Managing Tax Rates

Understanding your tax bracket is vital for effective tax management in the gig economy. The IRS uses a progressive tax system, and your income tax rate doesn't apply to every dollar you earn. It's essential to get familiar with the applicable tax brackets and rates to effectively plan and minimize your tax liabilities.

Using tax calculators available online can help with these calculations, but consider connecting with a certified public accountant (CPA) for personalized guidance.

8.6. Professional Tax Help

Navigating tax laws and obligations can sometimes feel complex and overwhelming. Don't shy away from seeking professional help. Hiring a CPA or tax advisor can provide crucial insight and expertise, ensuring you are leveraging all the available opportunities to minimize your tax liability.

A tax professional can also help you understand any changes in tax codes, which occur annually, so you can adjust your tax strategies accordingly. By seeking professional help, you not only receive expert advice but also save yourself the time and stress of managing complex tax processes alone.

8.7. Staying Abreast of Changing Tax Laws

Just as the gig economy itself evolves, so do the tax laws that govern it. Regularly keep abreast of tax revisions, either by following authoritative websites, subscribing to newsletters, or by maintaining regular contact with a tax professional.

Remember, staying informed can empower you to make the most tax-effective choices. An understanding of tax laws and the ability to navigate them effectively acts as a compass, guiding you towards financial success in the gig economy. Be proactive, diligent, and meticulous, and you'll see the depth of opportunities at your disposal to flourish and prosper.

Chapter 9. Saving Strategies for Financial Freedom

The road to financial freedom as a participant in the gig economy can seem daunting, but it needn't be. A key ingredient to achieving this is developing efficient saving strategies. To assist you in doing so, we will discuss a variety of techniques, ideas, and ways to strive towards financial growth and stability in your career as a modern gig worker.

9.1. Constructing Your Financial Framework

The first step towards effective saving is establishing a clear financial structure. Since income from the gig economy can be inconsistent, it is vital to have a solid financial framework.

To establish your financial framework, you need to set up various accounts dedicated to different categories of spending and saving. These could include an emergency fund, savings for tax payments, retirement savings, personal savings for goals such as vacations or house, and an account for daily expenses.

Let's break down each category:

1. Emergency Fund: This fund should be robust enough to cover three to six months' worth of living expenses. It should be easily accessible but not so accessible that it might encourage spontaneous spending.

2. Taxes: Many gig workers forget that they, as independent contractors, are solely responsible for their taxes. So, setting aside a percentage (generally 30%) of incoming payments for taxes is a wise move.

3. Retirement Savings: Pension plans are often non-existent for gig workers. It's up to you to plan for your retirement. Exploring options like a Simplified Employee Pension (SEP) or an Individual Retirement Account (IRA) is advisable.

4. Personal Savings: This involves saving for future personal goals or significant purchases, providing a roadmap for your life beyond the workforce.

5. Daily Expenses: This account will take care of your monthly needs, such as rent, utilities, groceries, and so on.

By segregating your finances, you can efficiently manage your money and ensure that regular expenses, emergencies, and long-term goals are all covered.

9.2. Imposing a Personal Pay Structure

Irregular income from gig jobs can make it challenging to manage your finances. One solution to this is to impose a personal pay structure.

Start by figuring out your bare minimum monthly living costs, including rent/mortgage, bills, food, and transportation. Then, pay yourself this bare minimum salary each month. Any additional income can be distributed among your other financial goals or saved for months when you might not make as much.

For example, suppose you earn $4000 in January, while your minimum monthly living cost is $2000. You can distribute the surplus $2000 among your other financial goals or save it for February, when you might earn less than your minimum requirement.

9.3. Consistently Tracking and Evaluating Your Spending

Tracking your spending is crucial to identify areas where you can cut back. There are several free apps that can help you monitor your expenditures and provide an overview of your spending habits.

Categories like dining, entertainment, shopping, and travel can significantly consume your budget. Evaluating and cutting back on these costs will help you save substantial amounts.

Consider adopting the 50/30/20 rule, popularized by U.S. Senator Elizabeth Warren. This rule simply means that 50% of your income goes towards needs, 30% towards wants, and the remaining 20% is saved. This split allows for a good balance of expenditure and savings.

9.4. Exploring Passive Income Streams

While saving and cutting back on spending is crucial, it's equally important to look for ways to earn more. As a gig worker, exploring passive income streams can provide a sturdy financial cushion, especially during leaner months.

You might consider investing in stocks, bonds, or real estate, for example, or setting up an online course related to your skills, or even writing an eBook. These approaches will earn you extra income over time, without needing ongoing effort.

9.5. Utilizing Financial Tools

There's an array of great tools out there that can help you manage your finances more effectively.

1. Budgeting apps: Apps like Mint or YNAB (You Need a Budget) can track your spending and provide valuable insights into where your money is going.

2. Automatic saving apps: Apps like Digit or Acorns automatically save small amounts of money regularly, helping you to save without even thinking about it.

3. Retirement calculators: Tools like NerdWallet's retirement calculator can help you determine how much you need to save for retirement based on your age, income, and retirement age.

These tools can simplify your financial management, give you a clear view of your present situation, and guide your financial goals.

By incorporating these saving strategies into your financial planning, you will not only secure your present but also your future in the gig economy. Remember, the idea is to harness the independence and flexibility provided by the gig economy and turn it into a unique strength. It takes some discipline, but with well-planned strategies, your journey to financial freedom becomes a lot more achievable.

Chapter 10. Insurance and Legal Considerations

In modern economies, insurance and legal considerations have positioned themselves as cornerstone topics. Their strategic usage becomes all the more crucial when we talk about the gig economy, an area of work where conventional boundaries are crossed and new risks are experienced. Here we aim to equip you with those essential knowledge facets that can protect you legally and via insurance, while also maximizing your financial prosperity.

10.1. Understanding Insurance Needs

The first step to becoming financially proficient in a gig economy is to understand and evaluate your insurance needs. As an independent worker, you aren't covered by an employer's insurance policy. Thus, having appropriate insurance is paramount. Depending on the nature of your work, you might need to consider various types of insurance like health, disability, liability, and professional insurance.

If you're providing a service, liability insurance can guard against lawsuits resulting from injuries or property damages. Alternatively, professional indemnity insurance is crucial for roles where advice is provided, offering protection if a client loses money due to perceived poor guidance.

If your gig work is your primary income source, disability insurance takes on increased importance. It would provide a portion of your income if you become temporarily disabled and are unable to work. Health insurance, of course, is a necessity for everyone, regardless of employment type.

10.2. Legal Requirements

Moving to legal considerations, the gig economy, due to its relative novelty, presents its own unique legal challenges. It is prudent to maintain an elevated awareness about contracts, employment classification, taxes and licenses associated with your gig work.

A well-drafted contract will lay down the terms and conditions of the project, preventing any future misunderstanding. Be vigilant when signing contracts and don't hesitate to consult with a lawyer if complexities arise. Explicate the project's scope, compensation, delivery timelines, termination conditions, and confidentiality clauses. Keep the original signed contract in safe custody and a digital backup.

Employment classification can have critical legal implications. Misclassification could lead to significant fines and back payment of employment taxes. Always ensure you understand your legal standing - are you an employee or an independent contractor?

As for taxation, gig income is taxable, and filing it correctly entails maintaining diligent records of your earnings and expenses. For U.S. based workers, if you earn more than $600 from a company, you should receive a 1099-MISC or 1099-K form. Be sure to understand the tax deductions available for gig workers, such as work-related travel, home office cost and any tools/software needed for the work. You may want to consult with a tax professional to ensure you don't miss out on any potential benefits.

Finally, ensure your gig work complies with relevant licenses and permits needed for your profession. Check with your city's local business licensing department for the relevant information.

10.3. Navigating the Health Insurance Landscape

Navigating health insurance can often be a daunting task. Seek out coverage that best fits your individual health situation, budget, and work condition. It's crucial to understand the difference between an 'on' and 'off' marketplace plan.

While most gig workers have to purchase insurance on their own, many are unaware that they could qualify for premium tax credits or subsidies to offset the expense. Check your eligibility for the same. You can opt for a high-deductible health plan if you primarily need insurance against serious illnesses or accidents. Such a plan paired with a health savings account (HSA) can be a tax-efficient way to cover medical expenses. Always remember, choosing the right health insurance plan can bring down potential out-of-pocket costs and provide access to necessary care.

10.4. Choosing the Right Insurance and Legal Protection

Choosing the right insurance plans and legal protection is a crucial decision for gig economy workers. Apart from adequately understanding your insurance needs, consider factors like premiums, network restrictions, and examining customer reviews before opting for an insurance plan.

Connect with a financial advisor or use online tools to compare various plans and understand their practical implications. Always remember that cheapest may not be the best. A plan with low premiums may have high deductibles, copayments or coinsurances. Look at the overall cost and the level of protection the insurance is offering before making a decision.

Similarly, the choice of legal protection would depend on the nature of your gig work, local laws and your potential risk areas. A robust contract, a thorough understanding of employment laws, correct tax filing and necessary licenses can significantly reduce your legal vulnerabilities.

With this, we wrap up our detailed discussion on insurance and legal considerations involved in the gig economy. Armed with this knowledge, we hope you are better prepared to navigate these waters, treading the fine line between risk and opportunity more confidently. The gig economy, with its flexibility and freedom, can sometimes appear daunting due to potential financial and legal risks. However, with the right tools, knowledge and expert advice, you can turn potential threats into unprecedented opportunities.

Chapter 11. Forging Your Path: Case Studies and Success Stories

The narrative landscape of the gig economy is populated with stories of people who have not just survived but thrived. These case studies shed light on the practical application of smart, resourceful financial strategies which might serve as a beacon for others navigating the freelance waters. So, let's dive into some real-life accounts, gleaning from their triumphs and turning points, in achieving financial stability and success.

11.1. A Stream of Mini Successes: Janet the Graphic Designer

Janet is a graphic designer based out of San Francisco who turned to freelancing after a decade-long corporate stint. Instead of seeking a couple of large projects every month, Janet focused on managing a steady stream of mini-projects. This approach aids in stabilizing the cash inflow volatility typical of the gig economy. Employing prudent negotiation skills, Janet set minimum rate limits to ensure profitability on each project. A commitment to prompt delivery and open communication bolstered her relationship with clients, thereby enhancing her opportunities for repeat business.

11.2. Diversification: A Multi-Dimensional Skillset

Next, we find Chicago-based Matthew, a Lyft driver who also teaches guitar in his spare time. Matthew's story brings the significance of a diversified income stream to the forefront. His rideshare driving covers his immediate expenses, and then the revenue from his tutoring sessions goes directly into his savings. This well-balanced approach to income generation demonstrates a great way to create a financial buffer for lean periods.

11.3. The Power of Online Platforms: Rachel's Success Story

Rachel, a freelance writer and editor from Atlanta, leveraged the reach of online platforms. Tapping into sites like Upwork and Freelancer, Rachel managed to create an international client base. This gave her an edge over local market fluctuations and exchange rate advantages on some projects. She also made it a point to reinvest a portion of her earnings into upskilling through online courses, ensuring her skills remain relevant and competitive.

11.4. Multiple Streams with Less Hassle: Steve's Property Investments

Meet Steve, an IT contractor from New York, who reinvested part of his project earnings into rental property. Steve found that the income generated from his investment became a stable secondary source, especially when his IT contracts were in low demand. This case illustrates the smart inclusion of passive income streams in one's revenue portfolio.

11.5. Importance of a Rainy Day Fund: The Case of Alyson

Alyson from Austin was a successful marketing consultant juggling multiple clients. However, during the 2020 pandemic, her contracts reduced drastically. Luckily, Alyson had saved three months' worth of living expenses as a safety net. This emergency fund saved her from financial stress, establishing the importance of a financial buffer for unexpected circumstances.

11.6. Utilizing Fringe hours: Paula's Story

Paula, a freelance web developer, made a mastery of maximizing her productivity during fringe hours. By working during the quiet, distraction-free hours, she managed to take on additional projects without compromising on the quality of her work. This strategy not only aided her earnings but also allowed the flexibility to cater to client needs across different time zones.

11.7. Protecting Your Interests: Liam's Insurance Strategy

Liam, an independent contractor, navigated his financial journey by choosing the right insurance policies. To protect himself against loss of income due to sickness or accident, he invested in disability income insurance. His case underscores the importance of financial planning in protecting one's income and assets.

With these inspirational real-life stories in mind, remember that every gig economy journey is unique. It's crucial to find your own path, forge your strategies, and weave your success story. In the following chapters, we will explore various proven strategies to manage finances effectively in the gig economy.

Take a note from Janet's steady stream of projects, Matthew's diversified income, Rachel's strategic use of online platforms, Steve's secondary passive income stream, Alyson's investment in a safety net, Paula's maximization of her fringe hours, and Liam's wise choice of insurance. Each success story is a testament to the possibilities that lie within the rapidly morphing expanse of today's gig economy.

www.ingramcontent.com/pod-product-compliance
Lightning Source LLC
Chambersburg PA
CBHW071047260726
48661CB00007B/3189